TERRIFIC TAILS

Hana Machotka

Morrow Junior Books   New York

For Louie and his
terrific tail

Printed in Hong Kong by South China Printing Company (1988) Ltd.

1 2 3 4 5 6 7 8 9 10

Library of Congress Cataloging-in-Publication Data
Machotka, Hana.   Terrific tails / Hana Machotka.   p.   cm. Summary: Describes different kinds of tails and how they are used by such animals as peacocks, dogs, monkeys, and beavers.
ISBN 0-688-04562-6 (trade). —ISBN 0-688-04563-4 (lib. bdg.)
1. Tail—Juvenile literature.   [1. Tail.   2. Animals—Habits and behavior.]   I. Title
QL950.6.M25   1994   599'.04'9—dc20   93-17687   CIP   AC

Acknowledgments
My photographs were taken at the Catskill Game Farm, Palenville, New York; Claws 'n' Paws Wild Animal Park, Hamlin, Pennsylvania; the Bronx Wildlife Conservation Center, New York City; and the Staten Island Zoo.

My thanks go to Dr. Annamarie Lyles, assistant curator of ornithology, and Pat Thomas, curatorial intern of mammals, at the Bronx Center for sharing their observations; Shirley Diamond and Tammy Walsh, aides to the wallabies at the Children's Zoo at the Bronx Center, for their special help; Dr. Allison Andors, ornithologist at the American Museum of Natural History in New York City, for once again generously sharing his expertise; and William Summerville, assistant curator at the Staten Island Zoo, for kindly sharing his knowledge of peacocks.

As ever, thanks to my editor, Andrea Curley, art director Barbara Fitzsimmons, and designer Jean Cohn for their excellent work and contributions.

Have you ever marveled at the many different kinds of tails animals have? A tail may be covered with hair, spines, scales, or feathers. It may be flat, long, round, fan shaped, or pointed. Have you ever wondered how these different tails might be important to an animal?

Long, colorful feathers grow on the upper part of the peacock's tail. Short, strong feathers underneath support these long feathers, holding them straight up when the peacock opens them. This display of feathers helps announce to females, or *peahens*, that the male is ready to mate. He shakes his long feathers with a loud rattling sound, making his availability known to females and staking out his territory to other males. As you look at the tails in this book, see if you can figure out how each animal uses its tail to help it survive.

A muscular tail that is used for swimming belongs to a . . .

CROCODILE

As this flexible, scaly tail sways from side to side in the water, it keeps the crocodile in one place even against a strong current. The tail can also propel the crocodile quickly, silently, and without making a ripple as it sneaks up on an animal that has come to the water for a drink. Then the crocodile grabs the animal's nose, knocks it off its feet with a blow of its tail, and eats the animal underwater.

Some female crocodiles use their tails to build their nests in the sand. Others keep the eggs moist by splashing water over them with their tails until they hatch.

A tail can be used as a signal by a . . .

DOG

Like a signal, a dog's tail conveys information to other dogs. A dog that is excited when meeting another dog wags its tail vigorously as a friendly greeting. A dog that feels frightened tucks its tail tightly between its legs to show that it doesn't want to fight. In a group of dogs, a dog that holds its tail very high in the air indicates to everyone that it is the leader. By using their tails to signal feelings and intentions, dogs help prevent fighting and injury when they get together.

A dog's tail also helps it to keep its balance as it runs after a stick or prey. The weight of the tail keeps the dog's body steady as it twists, dodges, and stops suddenly.

A tail that acts as a safety belt belongs on a . . .

MONKEY

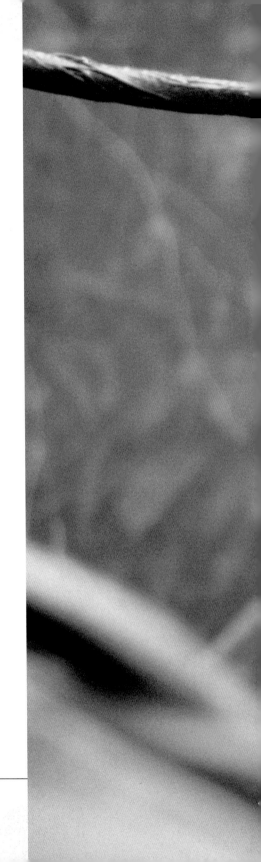

This spider monkey from South America has a *prehensile* tail that can grab and hold on to an object the way a hand does. When the monkey picks fruit from a tree with its front paws, the tail holds on to a branch for safety. As the monkey plays among the branches, the tail acts like an extra arm from which to swing. A spider monkey mother may wrap her tail around her baby for extra support as it rides on her back while she leaps among the branches.

The tip of the spider monkey's tail is hairless on the underside and is as sensitive to touch as your finger. It can find, probe, and pick up even small objects such as peanuts.

A sturdy tail that acts like a spring belongs on a . . .

WALLABY

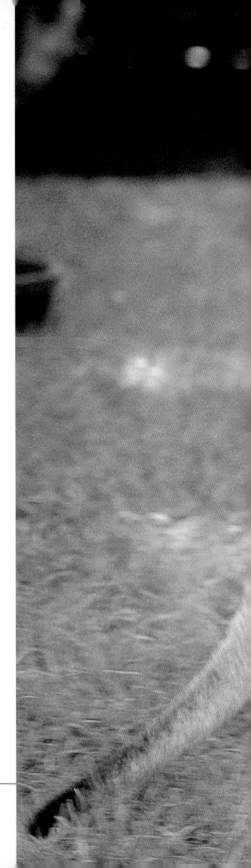

If a wallaby (a type of small kangaroo) had no tail, it could not jump or get around as quickly and easily as it does. The tail acts as a third leg, pushing the animal forward while its powerful hind legs leap up and over the tall grass. When walking, a wallaby cannot move one leg at a time as you do. It swings both hind legs forward while balancing its body on the tail and forelimbs.

When fighting, adult males sit back on their tails and legs to steady themselves. Then they box with their forelimbs, trying to knock each other off balance. A baby wallaby uses its tail and legs like a stool, sitting back on them as it nurses contentedly from its mother!

A flat, paddlelike tail with many uses is attached to a . . .

BEAVER

The beaver's unusual tail is covered with leathery scales and a few hairs. It can be used as a cushion to sit back on when the beaver is grooming its fur. In the water the tail wags back and forth to propel and steer the beaver, even if it is towing heavy logs and branches. When danger appears, the beaver raises its tail above the water and brings it down suddenly, making a sound like a pistol that warns other beavers far away.

Beavers cut down trees with their sharp teeth. They eat the green layer under the bark and use the wood to build homes in which to live. As it carries sticks and mud with its front paws, it waddles on its hind legs and balances with its wide tail. Sometimes mother beavers use their tails to ferry a baby over the water!

A long tail is an excellent balancing tool for a . . .

SNOW LEOPARD

The tail acts as a weight to balance the snow leopard's body as the cat leaps, stops, and turns suddenly. When the snow leopard is stalking prey, the tail stretches straight out behind to help keep the animal very still. Then the tail may twitch nervously just as the cat prepares to spring.

In freezing weather, the snow leopard can tuck its face under its furry tail, keeping its eyes covered and its nose warm. If snow falls while the cat is sleeping, the tail will keep the flakes off its face and give it breathing space.

This long, quick flyswatter is important to a . . .

HORSE

As they graze, horses flick their tails vigorously from side to side to help keep away flies that cause painful bites. In fact, a herd of horses often stands head to tail so that both ends of each horse are covered. Helping one another in this way strengthens bonds of friendship within a herd.

Horses also use their tails to show others how they feel. A tail held high shows that a horse feels alert and energetic. A tail held down shows that a horse is afraid, tired, or in pain. A violently swishing tail shows that a horse is annoyed and may kick—so look out!

A tail is much more than an interesting-looking body part. It is a very important appendage with a variety of uses. An animal that has lost its tail often cannot compete successfully in its environment.

Beavers and crocodiles both have scaly tails that are used for swimming. If the two animals exchanged tails, how would their lives change? If a cat and a horse switched tails, how would the cat's movements change—or the horse keep flies away?

When you look at animals in your neighborhood, at the zoo, or in a book, see how many different kinds of tails you can find. Can you figure out what each one can do?